Greater Than a Tourist Book Series
Reviews from Readers

I think the series is wonderful and beneficial for tourists to get information before visiting the city.

-Seckin Zumbul, Izmir Turkey

I am a world traveler who has read many trip guides but this one really made a difference for me. I would call it a heartfelt creation of a local guide expert instead of just a guide.

-Susy, Isla Holbox, Mexico

New to the area like me, this is a must have!

 -Joe, Bloomington, USA

This is a good series that gets down to it when looking for things to do at your destination without having to read a novel for just a few ideas.

-Rachel, Monterey, USA

Good information to have to plan my trip to this destination.

-Pennie Farrell, Mexico

Great ideas for a port day.

-Mary Martin USA

Aptly titled, you won't just be a tourist after reading this book. You'll be greater than a tourist!

-Alan Warner, Grand Rapids, USA

Even though I only have three days to spend in San Miguel in an upcoming visit, I will use the author's suggestions to guide some of my time there. An easy read - with chapters named to guide me in directions I want to go.

 -Robert Catapano, USA

Great insights from a local perspective! Useful information and a very good value!

 -Sarah, USA

This series provides an in-depth experience through the eyes of a local. Reading these series will help you to travel the city in with confidence and it'll make your journey a unique one.

-Andrew Teoh, Ipoh, Malaysia

GREATER THAN A TOURIST-TEXAS USA

50 Travel Tips from a Local

J.W. Wright

Cover designed by: Ivana Stamenkovic
Cover Image: https://pixabay.com/photos/rio-grande-river-texas-1581917/

Image 1: https://commons.wikimedia.org/wiki/File:Sam_Rayburn_Reservoir.jpg
Ricraider [CC BY-SA (https://creativecommons.org/licenses/by-sa/3.0)]
Image 2: https://commons.wikimedia.org/wiki/File:Texas_Hill_Country_187N-
2.JPG Zereshk [CC BY-SA (https://creativecommons.org/licenses/by-sa/3.0)]
Image 3:
https://commons.wikimedia.org/wiki/File:Palo_Duro_landscape_IMG_0101.JPG
Billy Hathorn at en.wikipedia [CC BY-SA
(http://creativecommons.org/licenses/by-sa/3.0/)]
Image 4: https://commons.wikimedia.org/wiki/File:Summitanthonysnose1b.jpg
I, Brian Stansberry [CC BY-SA (http://creativecommons.org/licenses/by-
sa/3.0/)]

CZYK Publishing Since 2011.
Greater Than a Tourist

Lock Haven, PA
All rights reserved.

ISBN: 9798613434602

>TOURIST

50 TRAVEL TIPS FROM A LOCAL

BOOK DESCRIPTION

With travel tips and culture in our guidebooks written by a local, it is never too late to visit Texas. Greater Than a Tourist - Texas by Author J.W. Wright offers the inside scoop on Texas culture, landmarks, and recreational activities. Most travel books tell you how to travel like a tourist. Although there is nothing wrong with that, as part of the 'Greater Than a Tourist' series, this book will give you candid travel tips from someone who has lived at your next travel destination. This guide book will not tell you exact addresses or store hours but instead gives you knowledge that you may not find in other smaller print travel books. Experience cultural, culinary delights, and attractions with the guidance of a Local. Slow down and get to know the people with this invaluable guide. By the time you finish this book, you will be eager and prepared to discover new activities at your next travel destination.

Inside this travel guide book you will find:

Visitor information from a Local
Tour ideas and inspiration
Save time with valuable guidebook information

Greater Than a Tourist- A Travel Guidebook with 50 Travel Tips from a Local. Slow down, stay in one place, and get to know the people and culture. By the time you finish this book, you will be eager and prepared to travel to your next destination.

OUR STORY

Traveling is a passion of the Greater than a Tourist book series creator. Lisa studied abroad in college, and for their honeymoon Lisa and her husband toured Europe. During her travels to Malta, an older man tried to give her some advice based on his own experience living on the island since he was a young boy. She was not sure if she should talk to the stranger but was interested in his advice. When traveling to some places she was wary to talk to locals because she was afraid that they weren't being genuine. Through her travels, Lisa learned how much locals had to share with tourists. Lisa created the Greater Than a Tourist book series to help connect people with locals. A topic that locals are very passionate about sharing.

TABLE OF CONTENTS

14. Western Wear
15. Buc-ee's

Food

16. Food Trucks
17. Crawfish
18. BBQ
19. Blue Bell
20. Tex-Mex
21. Whataburger
22. Fried Foods

Houston

23. Rothko Chapel
24. Space Center Houston
25. Cultural Festivals
26. Downtown Aquarium
27. Museums
28. Saint Arnold Brewing Company
29. Minute Maid Park
30. LGBTQ+ Destinations

DEDICATION

This book is dedicated to my family who gave me a love for adventure, my friends who encourage my wanderlust, and the beautiful state that I will always call home.

ABOUT THE AUTHOR

J.W. Wright is a writer who lives in Houston, Texas. He loves to travel, go camping, and take in the nightlife. As a history buff, he has a deep love for Texas' rich history and culture.

HOW TO USE THIS BOOK

The *Greater Than a Tourist* book series was written by someone who has lived in an area for over three months. The goal of this book is to help travelers either dream or experience different locations by providing opinions from a local. The author has made suggestions based on their own experiences. Please check before traveling to the area in case the suggested places are unavailable.

Travel Advisories: As a first step in planning any trip abroad, check the Travel Advisories for your intended destination.
https://travel.state.gov/content/travel/en/traveladvisories/traveladvisories.html

FROM THE PUBLISHER

Traveling can be one of the most important parts of a person's life. The anticipation and memories that you have are some of the best. As a publisher of the Greater Than a Tourist, as well as the popular *50 Things to Know* book series, we strive to help you learn about new places, spark your imagination, and inspire you. Wherever you are and whatever you do I wish you safe, fun, and inspiring travel.

Lisa Rusczyk Ed. D.
CZYK Publishing

WELCOME TO
> TOURIST

Sam Rayburn Reservoir

Texas Hill Country

Palo Duro Canyon

Franklin Mountains State Park

"Once the travel bug bites there
is no known antidote, and I know
that I shall be happily infected until
the end of my life."

– Michael Palin

John Steinbeck famously said that "Texas is a state of mind." It's hard to disagree with him. Texans are fiercely proud of our state and have created a culture unlike anything else in the world. Whether you're talking about food, fashion, or fun, it becomes quickly apparent that Texans tend to have our own way of doing things.

This can be somewhat intimidating for newcomers, but there's no need to fear! You'll find that the legendary "Southern Hospitality" is still very much alive in the Lone Star State. Texans are happy to share our culture with visitors and there's a very good chance that you won't want to leave.

Of course, it can be a bit intimidating when first visiting Texas. The 2018 U.S. Census had three Texas cities (Houston, San Antonio, and Dallas) in its list of the top ten highest populated cities with two more, Austin and Fort Worth, coming in at eleventh and thirteenth place respectively. Furthermore, the state is one of the largest in the US and is bigger than many countries! With so many people and so much space, it's not shocking that people can live their whole lives in Texas without seeing everything that it has to offer!

There is no shortage of amazing food, scenic nature, and exciting activities to enjoy while you visit. This guide will make sure that you're prepared to experience the state of mind that is Texas. It's only fair to warn you, though: there's a good chance that you may never want to leave! So, if you are reading this and have yet to have been greeted properly, please allow me to be the first to say "Howdy!"

Texas
United States

Austin
Texas
Climate

	High	Low
January	61	41
February	65	45
March	73	51
April	80	59
May	86	66
June	92	72
July	96	74
August	96	74
September	90	70
October	82	60
November	71	50
December	63	43

GreaterThanaTourist.com

Temperatures are in Fahrenheit degrees.
Source: NOAA

COMMON COURTESIES

"Texas is a blend of valor and swagger."

– Carl Sandburg

1. MANNERS ARE A MUST

Chivalry is alive and well in the Lone Star State. Be prepared to hear a great deal of manners such as "please", "thank you", "sir" and "ma'am" during your trip. Of course, it's important that you also use your manners well or you'll almost certainly find people staring.

2. SOUTHERN HOSPITALITY

Texans are known for being quick to be friendly towards others. Guests are quickly considered to be family and it's not uncommon for strangers to help each other in a pinch. In no time at all, you'll find yourself falling for our famous Southern charm.

3. HIGHWAYS

The Texas highway system is a true marvel and is vital to Texans' ability to travel large distances in a comparably short amount of time. Visitors may find the highways to be intimidating, but there is a method to the madness. The speed limit is a useful guide, but drivers should ultimately just keep pace with traffic. Only use the left-most lane when passing someone and be ready to politely move out of someone's way if they are going faster than you. Going the speed limit in the passing lane is a quick way to make the rules of Southern Hospitality no longer apply.

4. DON'T MESS WITH TEXAS

You would probably think that "Don't Mess with Texas" is our state's motto and, thanks to the Texas Department of Transportation's incredibly successful anti-littering campaign, you wouldn't be completely wrong. The slogan can be found all over Texas on road signs, TV commercials, and clothing. Texans are very proud of the natural beauty of our state and have very strict punishments for those who litter.

CULTURAL TIDBITS

"In Texas, we practically come out of the womb in jeans."

– Kelly Clarkson

5. SPEAKING TEXAN

Texans sometimes seem to have their own language. Fortunately, learning a few key phrases is all you need to find yourself quickly fitting in. A few particularly useful (and personal favorites) are:

- "Y'all" – Addressing multiple people, "you all"

o Ex. "It's so nice to meet y'all!"

- "Fixin' to…" – Someone is about to do something

o Ex. "I'm fixin' to book our hotel room for the trip."

- "Run to…" – To go somewhere

o Ex. "I'm fixin' to run to the store. Do ya'll need anything?"

- "Bless your heart!" – An expression that can be either an expression of empathy or an insult depending on how it's said.

29

o   Ex. "You haven't had chicken fried steak before? Bless your heart!"

o   Ex. "He still hasn't figured out how to park properly in that new truck. Bless his heart!"

6. EVERYTHING REALLY IS BIGGER IN TEXAS!

From Texans' personalities to our portion sizes, you will see why it is considered to be common knowledge that everything is truly bigger in Texas. To really experience this, you have to make time to visit the Texas State Fair which is held in Dallas every year from the last Friday of September through the middle of October. Don't be alarmed if you find a 55 feet tall cowboy greeting you with a booming "Howdy folks!" That's just Big Tex! He's the mascot of the State Fair and is a pretty big deal here!

7. FOOTBALL

Whether you're a sports fan or not, football is a religion in Texas. Whether it's professional football, college football, or high school football, we take it all pretty seriously. If you are trying to talk to somebody when the game is on, you may just want to wait until the commercial breaks.

8. MUSIC

Texas is a remarkably diverse state and our music scenes reflect that. Texans take a special pride in musicians that are from our state. Willie Nelson, Beyoncé, Buddy Holly, Selena, and more are etched deep in the hearts of Texans. Whether your music taste is in country, blues, rock, or something completely different, you are certain to find an abundance of shows that you will enjoy.

9. TEXANS MEASURE DISTANCE IN TIME

I'll never forget the way that a visitor looked at me several years ago when I gave him directions. Without thinking, I had told him that his destination was about thirty minutes down the freeway. He was visibly confused and asked me what I meant. In a state as big as Texas, it just doesn't make sense to count miles. Instead, we measure in hours.

10. TEXAS-SHAPED EVERYTHING

As you can already tell, Texans are incredibly proud of their state. We are the only state, to my knowledge, which puts their state's shape on virtually everything. We've got Texas-shaped belt buckles and jewelry, Texas-shaped décor, and it's not uncommon to smell breakfast cooking in a Texas-shaped waffle maker. Of course, this means that the only difficult thing about getting souvenirs from your visit is figuring out how you're going to carry it all!

11. DIVERSITY

Texas consistently ranks among the most diverse states in the U.S. This diversity traces all throughout Texas' history and is one of the reasons that Texan culture is so dynamic. Music, food, and more all benefit from Texas' diversity and have combined to create something truly unique. But what else would you expect from a state that has flown under six different flags? Spain, France, Mexico, the Republic of Texas, the Confederate States of America, and the United States of America have all held sovereignty over Texas territory.

12. RODEOS

Nothing compares to the sheer spectacle of a rodeo. The food, the music, and the sport all create an event unlike anything else. Expect to see bull riding, steer wrestling, rodeo clowns, and more. Rodeos frequently book very large musical acts and are a great way to see some of your favorite bands. While country music is the most common, it's not uncommon to see other acts such as KISS or Bruno

Mars as the main musical attraction. The only thing that could make this kind of event even better is some real Texas barbecue, which you'll find in abundance as rodeos very commonly include cook-offs.

13. BEER

Texans have a deep appreciation for beer and the explosion in popularity of craft beers in recent years has seen a colossal amount of breweries opening up across the state. Many of these breweries harken back to the tastes of Czech immigrants who defined much of central Texas in the old days. But don't be fooled! With so many breweries creating such a wide variety of beers, you're sure to taste flavors that you never thought were possible! Personally, I'm partial to the offerings from the Live Oak, 8th Wonder, and St. Arnold's breweries. When the Texas heat starts to beat down in summer, there is nothing like a cold Texan beer!

14. WESTERN WEAR

Few things are as iconic as the cowboy hat and boots. Wherever you go in Texas, you are certain to find stores with wide selections of Western clothing. There's nothing quite like a nice pair of boots and a well-made hat. You'll find that you can't help but have a bit of swagger in your step when you dress like a Texan.

15. BUC-EE'S

We have all been in this situation: you're on a long drive and become acutely aware that you need to use a restroom. You start looking for a convenience store and realize that you are also getting hungry. Where do you stop? A very large majority of Texans know the answer to this question.

Buc-ee's is a colossal convenience store that has become a verifiable symbol of Texas. It's so more than a gas station. With hundreds of gas pumps (no waiting!), the cleanest bathrooms that you have ever seen, and a shockingly massive selection of snacks and prepared foods, it's hardly a surprise that Buc-ee's has found itself with a devout following of customers. Go ahead and load up on their famous beef jerky and "Beaver Nuggets" (a crunchy corn puff snack). It's probably wise to grab one of their clever T-shirts while you're here. Once you've experienced the magic of a Buc-ee's location, you're certain to be back and tell your friends.

FOOD

"Only a rank degenerate would drive 1,500 miles across Texas without eating a chicken fried steak."

– Larry McMurtry

16. FOOD TRUCKS

Any big city in Texas will have fleets of food trucks offering unique foods for you to try. There are even parks where the food trucks all gather to make it even easier to sample multiple types of food. You'll find lots of interesting fusions of cuisines that you never thought were possible. Without a doubt, making it a point to visit some of the food trucks parked around town (typically outside of bars and events) is one of the quickest and most fun ways to learn the culinary tastes of Texas.

17. CRAWFISH

Being so close to Louisiana, crawfish (or mudbugs as they are also called) have become a favorite of Texans. Crawfish boils with friends and family are a tradition and numerous restaurants will happily advertise their crawfish specials during the season. A particular favorite of mine is the numerous Vietnamese-Cajun fusions available in Houston. The only thing better than crawfish is crawfish pho!

18. BBQ

The definitive food of Texas. Barbecue is more than just food to Texans. Families pass down recipes and techniques to making the perfect BBQ. Immediately upon arriving in Texas, you should locate the nearest BBQ restaurant. If we could, we would eat BBQ for breakfast, lunch, and dinner every day.

19. BLUE BELL

Sorry Ben & Jerry, but there's one undisputed ice cream in Texas: Blue Bell. Made in the town of Brenham (which is about halfway between Austin and Houston), Blue Bell ice cream has been a staple dessert for Texans since its founding in 1907. If you can take a trip to Brenham, it's definitely worth visiting the creamery. If you can't, you can still find Blue Bell ice cream at any grocery or convenience store. Your sweet tooth will thank you!

20. TEX-MEX

There's something magical about when two cultures combine to create something truly unique. This is especially true when it comes to food! While there are many things that I love about Texas, it would be fair to say that Tex-Mex is the primary reason that I can never stay away for too long. A magical assortment of cheese, spices, and beef define the cuisine. Texans can't help but be completely shocked by anyone who is able to resist the pure golden magic of chile con queso.

21. WHATABURGER

There's a clear favorite fast-food location among Texans: Whataburger. There's simply no comparison. It's easy to find yourself overwhelmed by the Texas-sized menu, but it's also impossible to make a bad decision. Find out why Whataburger is so loved by Texans!

22. FRIED FOODS

There is nothing that Texans can't fry. Some classics include chicken fried steak, fried pickles, and fried chicken. However, more unconventional foods such as fried ice cream and fried butter have been spotted at the Texas State Fair.

HOUSTON

"When I first arrived in Houston, I was fascinated with the elaborate styles of cowboy boots and thought they were incredibly exotic. They also seemed to be a central part of a specifically 'Texan' identity, one distinct from being 'American.'

– Shahzia Sikander

23. ROTHKO CHAPEL

One of my personal favorite locations in Houston is the Rothko Chapel. Since its creation in 1971, the Rothko Chapel has been a haven for reflection and meditation. People from all walks of life (including world leaders) have entered the chapel to reflect while admiring the murals inside.

The Rothko Chapel was founded by John and Dominique de Menil, of whom the nearby Menil Collection was named. The Chapel, itself, was named after the artist Mark Rothko. The paintings on the walls of the Chapel were all created by Rothko. Outside of the chapel is a distinct and fascinating sculpture by Barnett Newman, "Broken Obelisk," and a reflecting pool. With the Rothko Chapel's focus on social justice and freedom, it is only fitting that the statue is dedicated to Martin Luther King, Jr.

24. SPACE CENTER HOUSTON

Houston, we have no problems! Space Center Houston is the visitor center for NASA's famous Lyndon B. Johnson Space Center. Visitors get to see several space capsules and lunar modules displayed. One of my personal favorite stops is getting to see the Mission Control room for the International Space Station (ISS) and the preserved Apollo Mission Control.

One of the newest exhibits at Space Center Houston is the Mission Mars exhibit. Developed with NASA's help, it gives a fascinating glimpse into the work that NASA is currently doing to plan for future travel to Mars. In addition to the display of Mars rovers and a Mars meteorite (that you are allowed to touch!), it includes a virtual reality wall that creates a completely immersive experience for guests to learn about the future of space travel.

25. CULTURAL FESTIVALS

There is always something big going on in Houston. The cultural festivals are always a sight and create great opportunities to learn about other cultures. Enjoy the music, food, and art of people from the many diverse communities in Houston. Some personal favorites include the Polish Harvest Festival, Japan Festival, and Greek Festival.

Similarly, just north of Houston in the town of Todd Mission is the Texas Renaissance Festival. The Festival is an entire town with distinct areas showcasing food and performances from various cultures. Costumed performers tell jokes, play music, and perform remarkable stunts for the legions of guests that come each weekend over the nine week period.

26. DOWNTOWN AQUARIUM

The Downtown Aquarium is an absolute spectacle. It boasts a 500,000 gallon complex that includes rides (such as a Ferris wheel!) and a fantastic restaurant serving delicious surf-and-turf. The Downtown Aquarium is fun for the whole family and gives visitors a chance to see all manner of aquatic life. I especially enjoy the Shipwreck exhibit that takes place in the hull of a sunken Spanish galleon.

Interestingly, visitors to the Downtown Aquarium can see the Maharaja's Temple exhibit and its four White Tigers – Nero, Marina, Coral, and Reef. As of December 2019, the tigers have been moved to a massive 3,500 square-foot exhibit. Children will be especially excited for the "kid crawl" that allows them to get close to the Bengals! Watch as these beautiful cats climb, play, and sunbathe in the new exhibit that was specifically designed with the recommendations of carnivore experts from all over the US.

27. MUSEUMS

The city of Houston contains 19 different museums. The Menil Collection, Museum of Fine Arts, and others constantly have new exhibits on display for visitors to take in some of the best art in the world. The Holocaust Museum, Museum of African American Culture, and other similar museums offer opportunities for discovery-driven learning and cultural appreciation. Don't forget to also make time to visit the Houston Museum of Natural Science (especially the hypnotic and beautiful Cockrell Butterfly Center) and The Health Museum.

28. SAINT ARNOLD BREWING COMPANY

The Saint Arnold Brewing Company gives visitors a chance to see what goes into creating truly fantastic beer. Don't miss the chance to enjoy the Saint Arnold Beer Garden and Restaurant! It's a fantastic place to relax with some friends and you are allowed to bring games in. If you go during the week, make sure that you wear closed-toed shoes so that you can safely enter the downstairs portion of the tour and see the production process!

29. MINUTE MAID PARK

Minute Maid Park is the home stadium of the Houston Astros. There are few things that compare to enjoying a baseball game and Minute Maid Park is a great place to do so. Of course, the park has also hosted other events such as soccer, rugby, and professional wrestling. Additionally, the park has hosted concerts for performers including Paul McCartney, Madonna, Taylor Swift, and Beyoncé.

30. LGBTQ+ DESTINATIONS

The Montrose district is the hub for Houston's LGBTQ+ community and nightlife. Venues like South Beach, Rebar, and Blur Bar provide spacious dance floors and energetic settings in the heart of Montrose. If you're looking for a more relaxed side of the Montrose nightlife, Michael's Outpost has live pianists Wednesday through Sunday and Crocker Bar offers a relaxed, no-frills neighborhood environment.

DALLAS

"There is a special mystique to Texas. Texans represent many things to the uninitiated: We are bigger than life in our boots and Stetsons, rugged individualists who two-steppin' has achieved world-wide acclaim, and we were the first to define hospitality."

– Ann Richards

31. ARTS DISTRICT

The cultural hub of Dallas is a scenic district that is sure to excite you. The Meyerson Symphony Center and Winspear Opera House never fail to impress with their productions. The Dallas Museum of Art hosts many impressive exhibits showcasing art throughout the ages. I particularly recommend visiting the Nasher Sculpture Center. The sculpture garden spans nearly two acres and features a wide assortment of beautiful and intricate sculptures. The garden is a wonderful place to relax, reflect, and observe.

32. DEALEY PLAZA

Dealey Plaza is most infamously known as the location where President John F. Kennedy was assassinated in 1963. The Plaza is now home to the Sixth Floor Museum. The museum serves to chronicle the assassination of President Kennedy and preserve his legacy. This is a must-see for history buffs and is one of my favorite historical museums!

33. AT&T STADIUM

The home of the Dallas Cowboys, AT&T Stadium opened in 2009. The stadium is truly impressive and it is a fantastic experience for any visitor to attend a Cowboys game. As I said previously, football is a very big deal in Texas and the rush of the crowd is exhilarating!

The Stadium has also been used to host other events such as soccer (including the 2018 International Champions Cup), boxing, WrestleMania 32, and Supercross. Among the names of musicians who have performed at the AT&T Stadium, you will

find standouts including The Rolling Stones, George
Strait, Metallica, and Post Malone.

34. DALLAS ZOO

I absolutely love African wildlife and the Dallas
Zoo's "Giant of the Savanna" habitat is incredible.
Kids and adults alike will enjoy getting to feed the
elephants and giraffes. I most enjoyed watching the
gorillas and chimpanzees!

It's also worth checking out the "Koala
Walkabout" section. The Dallas Zoo has the only
koalas in Texas! You'll also be able to see other
Outback wildlife up close including the wallabies,
kangaroo, and lorikeets!

35. FAIR PARK

My absolute favorite happening in Dallas is the
Texas State Fair. Each fall, crowds come from far and
wide to attend the famous State Fair, ride the rides,
and eat the best (and craziest!) food that you've ever
heard of. No matter what, you can't leave until you
get one of the famous funnel cakes and a corn dog.

If you don't find yourself there in time for the Texas State Fair, there are still other events that happen every year at the park! In March, the North Texas Irish Festival lasts for three days over the first weekend of the month. If you find yourself in Dallas in time for July 4th, you owe it to yourself to see the Independence Day celebration! Much like the Texas State Fair, there is a huge spectacle of rides, music, food, and games to be enjoyed in celebrating Independence Day at Fair Park Fourth.

36. DALLAS FARMERS MARKET

There's something thrilling about the Dallas Farmers Market. Maybe it's the hustle and bustle mixed with the smell of fresh produce and soil. Maybe it's the way the humble Shed pavilion helps consumers meet farmers in a type of urban oasis beneath the massive Dallas skyscrapers. There is no better place in Dallas to get ahold of fresh produce, local specialties, and the best meat you will ever eat.

37. SIX FLAGS OVER TEXAS

The Texan answer to Disneyland, I can't help but feel slightly spoiled for growing up so close to the park. Keeping with the theme that "everything is bigger in Texas," Six Flags has a wide selection of rides that are sure to appeal to all levels of thrill-seeker. Kids especially will enjoy seeing the prevalence of Looney Tunes and DC Comics characters.

Six Flags also hosts incredibly fun seasonal events throughout the year. March marks the Spring Break Out event and sees the park adding more outdoor attractions and live music performances. In April, Six Flags celebrates Hispanic and Latino heritage with crafts, music, dancing, and special food options. It's impossible not to smile when you try one of the churros! The Festival Latino is one of the most vibrant special events that you could attend!

October marks the beginning of Fright Fest at Six Flags and is a truly impressive event. Spooky music is played as ghouls roam the park. If you are feeling brave, take advantage of the haunted houses!

Though we certainly can't forget the most popular seasonal event: Holiday in the Park. From the end of November through December, Six Flags becomes a verifiable winter wonderland. Special holiday shows and crafting activities are available (including an authentic snow hill that you can sled down!), but, in my opinion, the most enchanting part of the event is the lights. It's always a work of art and one can't help but be hypnotized by the myriad of lights.

38. DALLAS ARBORETUM & BOTANICAL GARDEN

On the shore of White Rock Lake is the Dallas Arboretum and Botanical Garden. The Arboretum is an incredible 66-acre piece of Heaven with 19 different named gardens to explore. There is no better place to take in the beauty of southern flora. I'm particularly fond of the Jonsson Color Garden and its incredible display of countless varieties of azaleas, daffodils, tulips, and seasonal flowers. The Arboretum constantly has special events and activities to attend as well. Some standouts are the Food and Wine Festival, Dallas Blooms, and gourmet cooking classes.

AUSTIN

"There is a freedom you begin to feel the closer you get to Austin, Texas."

— Willie Nelson

39. KEEP AUSTIN WEIRD

One of the first things that you will notice about Austin is the proudly displayed "Keep Austin Weird." Austin has a reputation for being a proud bastion for all things strange and counter-culture. This has created a unique culture that is unlike any other. You'll find this quirky charm all over the city and evident in such attractions as the "Cathedral of Junk" and the featured homes of the "Weird Homes Tour."

Keeping with the matra of "Keep Austin Weird," one will quickly come to find the abundance of local businesses. While there are some familiar chains for restaurants and shopping, Austinites are proud to support local businesses. This has resulted in some truly remarkable and unusual businesses.

With all of this forming the backdrop for Austin's official motto and claim as the "Live Music Capital of the World," there is never a shortage of "weird" things to do. On any given night, a cornucopia of (usually free!) live music performances can be attended in any of the hundred-plus venues in the city. Additionally, Austin is home to some of the largest music festivals in the world including South by Southwest (SXSW), Austin City Limits Music Festival (ACL), The Urban Music, and more!

40. TEXAS STATE CAPITOL

In downtown Austin, the Texas State Capitol is the seat of Texas government. With fascinating architecture and a rich history, the Texas Capitol is a must-see when visiting Austin. Tours are totally free and offer a great way to learn about Texas history and traditions. Fun fact: the Texas State Capitol building is the largest capitol building in the United States!

41. BULLOCK TEXAS STATE HISTORY MUSEUM

Just a few blocks north of the Texas State Capitol building is the Bullock Texas State History Museum. The museum puts a heavy focus on the evolving "Story of Texas" and features an assortment of fascinating exhibits. Named after the 38th Lieutenant Governor of Texas, Bob Bullock, the Bullock Museum has worked tirelessly to chronicle Texas history since its establishment in 2001.

Perhaps most remarkable is the "Becoming Texas" exhibit on the first floor. "Becoming Texas" offers an immersive journey through over 16,000 years of Texas history and in-depth discovery of the early people who lived in the region up to Mexican Independence in 1821. This look into history provides an incredible foundation for the other exhibits and will give you an incredible understanding of what it means to be a Texan.

42. DINOSAUR PARK

Only a few miles from the Austin Bergstrom International Airport is Cedar Creek. Cedar Creek is home to the Dinosaur Park and should be a high priority visit if you have children. Tickets are very inexpensive and the assortment of dinosaur statues along the walking path are sure to excite! Be sure to also take advantage of activities such as digging for fossils, the playground, and picnic area!

43. BROKEN SPOKE

No list of fun things to do in Austin is complete without mentioning the incredible music scene. No dance hall in Texas compares to Broken Spoke and one needs only to walk through the front door to get a sense of the importance of dance halls to Texas culture. Don't know how to Two-Step? Broken Spoke has dance lessons four days a week that will get you ready for the dancefloor in no time at all! While you're there, be sure to try the Chicken Fried Steak for some of the best Texas food you'll find!

44. CONGRESS AVENUE BRIDGE BAT-WATCHING

What's not to love about bats? The Congress Avenue Bridge over Lady Bird Lake is home to North America's largest urban bat colony. Over one million Mexican free-tail bats emerge nightly from late March through early November to take flight and forage for food. By far one of the most fascinating (and unusual) activities that Austin has to offer, the sight of the bats against the orange sky in the evenings makes for a fantastic photo opportunity. Boat tours provide the best view of the colony, though the colony can also be viewed from the bridge itself or from the Lady Bird Lake trail on the South side of the lake.

45. MUSEUM OF THE WEIRD

Austin's Sixth Street is legendary for those seeking to party, but one particular location on Sixth Street has long held my interest: Lucky Lizard Curios and Gifts. Not only is this store truly weird (in the coolest of ways!), but it is also home to one of the last "dime museums" in the U.S. These museums trace back to the legendary P.T. Barnum in the 19th century and went on to form the famous sideshows that so frequently traveled with the circus.

I have a deep love for freak-shows and there is nowhere else that I would expect such a trove of things that can only be described as… well… weird! Sasquatch footprints, shrunken heads, mummies and more await visitors. Before you go to experience the parties on Sixth Street, you simply must visit the Museum of the Weird!

46. BIG TOP CANDY SHOP

If you've got a sweet tooth, Big Top Candy Shop is the premiere destination in Austin for candies, soda, and ice cream. They have a jaw-dropping mixture of candies both new and retro. If you're a fan of saltwater taffy, their variety will blow your mind! Candies in all shapes, sizes, and flavors await your discovery. Oh, and you haven't lived until you've tried their Double Bacon Chocolate Bar.

When's the last time that you had a soda made by a soda jerk? Big Top offers old-fashioned hand-jerked sodas in over thirty different flavors. On especially hot days, you'll definitely want to visit to try one of their shakes or malts. The shakes are made with Blue Bell ice cream and are some of the best that you'll find anywhere!

SAN ANTONIO

"That's why I like Texans so much. They took a great failure and turned it into a tourist destination that makes them millions. Texans don't bury their failures. They get inspired by them."

– Robert T. Kiyosaki

47. THE RIVER WALK

Along the San Antonio River are the parks and walkways that make up the San Antonio River Walk. The best way to experience San Antonio is by taking a cruise on the River Walk which are pleasantly very affordable. The River Walk allows you quick access to visit many of the city's historical sites (including the famous Alamo), take in the rich flavors of the many restaurants in the city, and shop. At over 2 miles long, it is very easy to spend an entire day on the River Walk!

48. THE ALAMO

The battle cry "Remember the Alamo!" has cemented itself in history and pop culture. It was originally a mission that became the site of one of the most important battles of the Texas Revolution. As the Texan revolutionaries fought to the very last man before being defeated by the Mexican army, the Alamo became a symbol of the Revolution and the Texan spirit in the counterattacks that would follow. Today, the Alamo maintains its status as a symbol for the state and is one of the premiere destinations for tourists in Texas.

49. MISSION SAN JOSÉ

Known as the "Queen of the Missions," Mission San José is a late 18th century Catholic mission in San Antonio. It is one of five missions that have been designated as "World Heritage Sites" by the United Nations Education, Scientific, and Cultural Organization. The mission turns 300 years old in 2020 and is still committed to preserving the details of the indigenous people during the colonial period while also celebrating the vibrant cultures present in San Antonio today.

50. NATURAL BRIDGE WILDLIFE RANCH

As I mentioned earlier, I have a deep fascination by African wildlife. For this reason, I cannot recommend the Natural Bridge Wildlife Ranch enough. As a wonderful mix of education and preservation, the Ranch is traveled as a safari. Giraffes, zebras, ostriches and more abound. I particularly enjoy visiting the lemurs in the Lemur Island area! Make sure to take your kids by the petting barn where they can visit the African pygmy goats!

BONUS TIP 1: NATURAL BRIDGE CAVERNS

The Natural Bridge Caverns are the largest known commercial caverns in Texas. You will be hypnotized by the beautiful formations inside the caverns. Multiple tour options are available and I highly recommend arriving early for the Lantern Tour. The Lantern Tour is the first tour of the day and you will navigate the caverns by lantern. If you prefer to get dirty, an Adventure Tour is offered that allows you to climb, crawl, and rappel as you explore the caverns that are untouched by walkways and lighting.

On the surface, there are multiple other attractions that are fun for the whole family. The Twisted Trails course offers a scenic view of the Texas Hill Country as you navigate a sixty-foot high course of ropes and zip rails. Dig for treasure in the Gem and Fossil Mining activity or test your strength in the climbing challenges!

BONUS TIP 2:
JAPANESE TEA GARDEN

In my opinion, the most beautiful place to visit in San Antonio is the Japanese Tea Garden in Brackenridge Park. It was previously a quarry, but is now a monument to the beauty of Japanese culture. This peaceful garden features incredible stonework, koi ponds, and a vast array of exotic plants.

Look out for regular events at the Japanese Garden. Live music events are hosted throughout the year and always include food and games that the whole family can enjoy. The Fest of Tails is an annual kite festival and is definitely something to check out. The kites of all designs form a bouquet of color that is sure to spark joy!

OTHER DESTINATIONS

"For a few precious moments…
I'm back in Old Texas, under a high
sky, where all things are again
possible and the wind blows free."

– Larry L. King

BONUS TIP 3:
SOUTH PADRE ISLAND

If you find yourself in south Texas and want to check out the waters of the Gulf of Mexico, South Padre Island is the place to go! While there are many exciting coastal cities, South Padre Island is a paradise. Dolphin watching, parasailing, fishing, and more mean that there is always plenty of beach fun to be had.

Be warned: South Padre is one of Texas' premiere Spring Break destinations. In March, huge masses come to the island to party and celebrate over Spring Break. If you're not looking for a party, you may want to avoid the island in March!

BONUS TIP 4:
JACOB'S WELL

Thrill-seekers will take an interest in the opportunity to dive into Jacob's Well. Jacob's Well is a legendary spring located in the Texas Hill Country that surfaces through a hole that is only twelve feet wide. Because of the surrounding aquifer, the water stays clear and cool (around 68 degrees) at all times of the year. In the often-brutal summer heat, it's a great way to cool off!

Don't be fooled though! Diving into the well leads into an underwater cave system that is over 120 feet deep. Jacob's Well is well-known for the dangerous nature of the caves. With tight corners, sharp angles, and narrow passageways, this is not an adventure for the faint of heart.

BONUS TIP 5:
BIG BEND NATIONAL PARK

With more than 800,000 acres of desert, mountain range, and river, Big Bend National Park offers some of the greatest views and most challenging climbs that you could ever experience. See the beauty of the Rio Grande River that forms the border between Texas and Mexico. As an interesting note, the entire twenty mile Chisos mountain range is contained within the park. No other park in the United States contains an entire mountain range!

With some of the best scenery in Texas and a massive expanse that is just waiting to be explored, you could easily spend several days in the park and only scratch the surface of what it has to offer. Be sure to bring a camera because this is Texas' scenery at its most majestic.

BONUS TIP 6: FREDERICKSBURG

Among the many distinct cultures that have combined to shape Texas, one cannot forget the rich German heritage that is still present in central Texas to this day. Fredericksburg is a prime example of this heritage and is a prime destination within the Texas Hill Country.

With such a scenic location, the only thing that could make it better is a nice glass of wine. Fortunately, Fredericksburg has over fifty wineries and tasting rooms to visit. I'm particularly a fan of both the Messina Hof and Signor Vineyards wineries.

Enchanted Rock is a must-visit for camping, hiking, and picnicking. A curious feature of the dome is its tendency to make groaning and creaking sounds. While the legends claim these sounds to be caused by ghosts, Texas Parks and Wildlife states that the sounds are due to changes in temperature. It's up to you to decide!

BONUS TIP 7: GALVESTON

I have a deep love for Galveston. From the Victorian mansions and historic sites to the vibrant nightlife found on The Strand, Galveston has something for everyone. Moody Gardens is a standout place to visit while you're on the island for a truly unique experience within the eye-catching pyramids showcasing aquariums, rainforests, and more!

You will find a major pirate theme around the island as Galveston's history a major port for pirates is an infamous part of its history. For those with an interest in pirate history, Galveston is a treasure trove! The infamous French pirate, Jean Lafitte, once lived on the island and the ruins of his Maison Rouge are a major attraction for ghost hunters.

Embracing the island's Victorian history, anyone near Galveston should make it a point to visit the annual Dickens on the Strand event. The first weekend of December sees the Strand travel back in time to Victorian London to channel Charles Dickens and his classic "A Christmas Carol." Witness the parades, four stages of entertainment, and characters that make Dickens on the Strand such a standout event. Even better, if you happen to have a Victorian costume handy, admission is free!

BONUS TIP 8: MARFA

A small city in the west Texas desert has become one of the state's best-kept secrets. With a population of less than 2,000 people, Marfa has become a hub for the arts. The famous minimalist artist, Donald Judd, moved to this quiet desert town in the 1970s and acquired an Army base. He immediately set to filling it with art and founded The Chinati Foundation. Chinati specifically intends to preserve and present art installations that link with the surrounding landscape. One such example is "Prada, Marfa." The sight of a Prada boutique (unstaffed, I'm afraid) displaying luxury goods against the desert background creates a distinct sense of fascination with the clash of images. As an artistic oasis in the plains of the Chihuahua desert, Marfa is sure to leave you speechless!

Film buffs may be interested to know that the film "Giant" starring Elizabeth Taylor and Rock Hudson was filmed in Marfa. Meanwhile, those with a passion for unsolved mysteries will certainly want to keep an eye out at night for the famous Marfa Lights. The lights appear as large glowing orbs and have fascinated people since their first known mention in the late 1800s. Ghosts? Aliens? Something else entirely? The world may never know.

BONUS TIP 9: BLUEBONNETS

It would be a sin to not mention the state flower of Texas: the bluebonnet. Fields of bluebonnets can be found all over the state in spring. Ennis (just south of Dallas) is designated as the official bluebonnet city of Texas and has one of the best bluebonnet trails in the state. Just outside of Brenham, mid-way between

Houston and Austin, Chappell Hill is another prime location to see the bluebonnets in bloom. Just northwest of Austin is the city of Burnet. In April, Burnet becomes the site of the annual Bluebonnet Festival which features live music, a parade, a demolition derby, and so much more.

BONUS TIP 10: NEWMAN'S CASTLE

When you think of Texas, several images likely come to mind. You likely think of cowboys, cattle, or country music. What about a medieval castle?

In the small town of Bellville, a baker by the name of Mike Newman has built a magnificent castle. Newman's Castle is complete with a moat, drawbridge, and trebuchets. In a style that one would expect from any eccentric Texan, Newman's Castle has stood out to become one of the most fantastic curiosities in Texas.

Because the castle is a private residence, you will need to make a reservation in advance. Simply call the bakery to reserve a date! Oh, and, don't forget to try the incredible donuts while you're there!

BONUS TIP 11:
THE (TEXAS) EIFFEL TOWER

While you're in Texas, you have to take a trip to Paris! That's right! Just northeast of Dallas is the city of Paris, Texas. As one would expect, the city is home to a Texas-style Eiffel Tower.

What makes the tower Texas-style? The cowboy hat resting on top of it, of course! Funnily enough, another Eiffel Tower was unveiled the same year as the one in Texas in the city of Paris, Tennessee. The tower in Tennessee stood five feet higher than its Texas counterpart. Not to be outdone, the now-iconic cowboy hat that rests atop the tower was added 3 years later to overtake the height of the Tennessee tower.

BONUS TIP 12: MINERAL WELLS FOSSIL PARK

Just west of Dallas lies the city of Mineral Wells. Famous for its Fossil Park, rockhounds and paleontologists will want to visit this site. Once a landfill, the Fossil Park is overflowing with all manner of 300 million year old fossils. The best part? You get to keep what you find!

Fossils include all manner of plants, sea urchins, sharks, and more! You'll want to be sure to bring plenty of water (especially in the famously brutal Texas summer) and bags to hold your findings. As a tip, the best time for fossil hunts are after it rains or storms!

BONUS TIP 13: CADILLAC RANCH

Among the strange and fascinating art displays that one can find off the beaten path in Texas, the Cadillac Ranch is particularly famous. Ten Cadillacs are partially buried nose-down in a stretch of a dusty Texas field. Emerging from the ground as a type of automobile-themed Stonehenge, the cars are covered in layers of graffiti. Don't worry though! That's very much the point! The Cadillac Ranch is open to the public at all hours and every visit to the Ranch results in a new artistic experience. You may also enjoy the nearby and similarly-themed VW Slug Bug Ranch that features – you guessed it! – the iconic Volkswagen Beetles buried nose-down in the ground and waiting to be covered in more spray paint!

BONUS TIP 14:
TUBING ON ANY RIVER

Summers in Texas can get brutal and it's important to know how the locals cool off! One of the biggest rites of passage for any visitor to Texas is to go river tubing. Texas is home to some of the most beautiful rivers in the country and there is no better way to cool off on a hot day than floating downstream in a tube.

The most popular tubing destination is in the Texas Hill Country on the Guadalupe River. Floats here can range from two to six hours! A personal favorite is the Frio River in Garner State Park. As the name implies, the Frio River ("Frio" mean "cold" in

Spanish) stays nice and cool. The long, scenic float is perfect for a hot summer day! But, as Texans love to float on the rivers, there are certainly tubing options available!

BONUS TIP 15: EXPLORE TEXAS' CZECH ROOTS

Few things will make a Texan's ears perk up faster than mentioning "kolaches." With the influx of Czech immigrants to Texas in the 19th century, all manner of delightful pastries and beers became Texas staples. With particular concentrations in Central Texas, the influence of these immigrants is still alive and well today. The city of West lies between Waco and Dallas and is filled with Czech flavors. The kolaches at the "Czech Stop" in West are among the best I've ever had and if there were ever a reason to venture off the beaten path, this would be it. Similar gems can be found in Weikel's in La Grange and Hruska's in Ellinger. Fortunately, La Grange and Ellinger are both close enough to each other on the trip between Austin and Houston that one can easily sample the Czech delights in both!

BONUS TIP 16: DIXIE DUDE RANCH

Northwest of San Antonio is Bandera, Texas. No guide to Texas would be complete without mentioning a ranch. Nestled in the beauty of the Texas Hill Country, the Dixie Dude Ranch stands tall as one of the best places to stay and enjoy the cowboy lifestyle. A wide range of activities are available for the whole family including horseback riding, fishing, and hayrides.

The Ranch is also close to many other fun activities to ensure that you get the most out of your stay. With several venues for music and dancing in Bandera, you'll be able to take in the nightlife western-style. Furthermore, you will be very close to the Guadalupe, Frio, and Medina rivers which makes for great tubing and kayaking opportunities!

TEXAN-ISMS

*"If a man's from Texas, he'll tell
you. If he's not, why embarrass him
by asking?"*

– John Gunther

"I must say as to what I have seen of Texas, it is the garden spot of the world. The best land and best prospects for health I ever saw is here, and I do believe it is a fortune to any man to come here. There is a world of country to settle." – Davy Crockett

Texans love our expressions and it can be confusing to visitors. Below are some of the most common expressions that you are likely to hear when visiting the Lone Star State. Even better, you'll get some major bonus points if you use these as well!

Texan-ism #1:
"All hat and no cattle" or "Big hat, no cattle"
Translation:
Someone who is all talk with no action.
Example:
"That restaurant says they have the best chili in
    Texas, but I think they're all hat and no cattle."

Texan-ism #2:

"Madder than a wet hen."

Translation:

Incredibly angry

Example:

"He was madder than a wet hen when he realized that he left his wallet at home before going to the grocery store."

Texan-ism #3:

"This ain't my first rodeo."

Translation:

"I have experience with this."

Example:

"I assured the team at my new job that this ain't my first rodeo."

Texan-ism #4

"I reckon"

Translation:

"I guess" or "I think"

Example:

"I reckon we'll try that new steakhouse this weekend."

Texan-ism #5

"Come hell or high water"

Translation:

"No matter what"

Example:

"I told my best friend that I'll be at her wedding come
hell or high water."

Texan-ism #6

"You can hang your hat on"

Translation:

To trust, believe, or rely on something. It can also be
used to describe a place that you can call home."

Examples:

"Jeff can hang his hat on his ability to make new
friends."

"If you're looking for a place to hang your hat, you
might want to look at moving to Texas."

Texan-ism #7

"More than you can shake a stick at"

Translation:

A large amount of something, abundance

Example:

"There are more bats under the Congress Avenue
Bridge in Austin than you can shake a stick at!"

Texan-ism #8

"Might could"

Translation:

Possibly able to

Example:

"I might could give you a ride to the concert tonight."

Texan-ism #9

"That dog won't hunt"

Translation:

"That won't work"

Example:

"He made a submarine with a screen door, but that
dog won't hunt."

Texan-ism #10

"Putting lipstick on a pig"

Translation:

Trying to disguise something or make it seem fancier
than it really is.

Example:

"I was considering buying that used car, but the
salesman kept trying to put lipstick on a pig."

TOP REASONS TO BOOK THIS TRIP

"There was a vastness here, more air, more sun, more space, and I thought that here a man drew some of that vastness into his soul. They dream big dreams and think big thoughts because there is nothing to hem them in." – Conrad Hilton

Food:

The food is unlike anything else in the world. With a such a rich mix of vibrant cultures, Texas does food in a way that only Texas could. Barbecue, seafood, Tex-Mex, and more are staples in any town or city regardless of its size. Be sure to bring your appetite because, as the saying goes, "Everything is Bigger in Texas" and that is especially true for the portion sizes.

Culture:

With a rich cultural heritage, deep appreciation for its history, and a bold attitude that shapes its future, Texas is a cultural epicenter. There is a reason that the Texan attitude is known all over the world. You'll find that it's easy to make friends with Texans and that nearly every one that you meet will be happy to recommend the best places to visit in the state.

Scenery:

As one of the largest states in the United States, Texas is home to a plethora of some of the most beautiful scenery in the country. We take a great deal of pride in the landscapes that adorn our state and work tirelessly to preserve them and our wildlife. Texas is a dream come true for avid hikers, campers, and lovers of the outdoors.

DID YOU KNOW?

"You can take the girl out of Texas but not the Texas out of the girl." – Janine Turner

1. The name "Texas" is derived from the Spanish pronunciation of the Hasinai word for "friend": "táysha'"
2. Texas still owns all of its public land. This means that the US Federal Government must ask permission to create a park or cut timber.
3. Houston is the largest city in Texas and is the 4th largest city in the US.
4. Texas was its own country, The Republic of Texas, for 10 years (1836-1845) prior to being annexed by the United States.
5. The Texas state bird is the mockingbird. The mockingbird is also the state bird for Florida, Tennessee, Arkansas, and Mississippi.
6. The Dallas-Fort Worth airport is larger than the island of Manhattan in New York.
7. The city of Tyler is home to the Tyler Municipal Rose Garden. With over 38,000 rose bushes and 500 varieties of roses, it is the largest rose garden in the world.

8. Some famous Texans include Buddy Holly (musician), Dwight D. Eisenhower (34th US President), Bonnie Parker and Clyde Barrow (famous outlaws), and Janis Joplin (musician).

9. In Norway, "Texas" is a slang word that means that something is wild or crazy. (Ex. a party that is totally Texas!)

10. Texas has over 72,000 miles of highways. The Katy Freeway at Beltway 8 in Houston is the world's widest freeway with 26 lanes!

11. The city of Athens, Texas claims to be the place where the world's first hamburgers were created in the late 1880's.

TRIVIA (JUST FOR FUN!)

"Texas is the finest portion of the globe that has blessed my vision."

– Sam Houston

1) What is the Texas State nickname?
2) What is the official Texas State animal?
3) Who was the first president of the Republic of Texas?
4) Who was the Mexican general who fought against the Texas Revolution?
5) What popular soft drink was invented in Waco, Tx in 1885?
6) What is the name of the official state song of Texas?
7) Complete this lyric: "The stars at night, are big and bright…"
8) What is the official motto of Texas?
9) Texas is one of only seven states that do not have a what?
10) What food is the State Dish of Texas?

ANSWERS

1) The Lone Star State

2) Armadillo

3) Sam Houston

4) Santa Anna

5) Dr Pepper

6) "Texas, Our Texas"

7) "Deep in the heart of Texas" (Bonus points if you
   did the famous claps!)

8) "Friendship"

9) State income tax

10) Chili

FINAL THOUGHTS

It is my most sincere hope that you enjoy your visit through Texas. Like so many other Texans, I am proud to call it my home and I appreciate this opportunity to share some of our culture with you. We tend to be loud and some may say that we take a little too much pride in our identity, but I truly believe that you can find anything you want in the Lone Star State.

We are a people that were born through revolution and a rugged sense of individualism. Our reputation and culture is known worldwide through film, music, and literature. Texas has been the epicenter of some of the world's most incredible human achievements. As the only state to enter the United States via treaty and not annexation, we have a sense of respect for others that is easily shown but difficult to express. It's a firm handshake, a tip of the hat, and a friendly smile.

Texas is a place where you can truly find who you are and become it. You'll always find a home and plenty of amazing food in any of the cities that make up our dynamic culture. You may come to Texas as a tourist, but I have no doubt that you will leave it as something greater: a friend.

PACKING AND PLANNING TIPS

A Week before Leaving

- Arrange for someone to take care of pets and water plants.

- Email and Print important Documents.

- Get Visa and vaccines if needed.

- Check for travel warnings.

- Stop mail and newspaper.

- Notify Credit Card companies where you are going.

- Passports and photo identification is up to date.

- Pay bills.

- Copy important items and download travel Apps.

- Start collecting small bills for tips.

- Have post office hold mail while you are away.

- Check weather for the week.

- Car inspected, oil is changed, and tires have the correct pressure.

- Check airline luggage restrictions.

- Download Apps needed for your trip.

Right Before Leaving

- Contact bank and credit cards to tell them your location.

- Clean out refrigerator.

- Empty garbage cans.

- Lock windows.

- Make sure you have the proper identification with you.

- Bring cash for tips.

- Remember travel documents.

- Lock door behind you.

- Remember wallet.

- Unplug items in house and pack chargers.

- Change your thermostat settings.

- Charge electronics, and prepare camera memory cards.

READ OTHER GREATER THAN A TOURIST BOOKS

Greater Than a Tourist- Geneva Switzerland: 50 Travel Tips from a Local by Amalia Kartika

Greater Than a Tourist- St. Croix US Birgin Islands USA: 50 Travel Tips from a Local by Tracy Birdsall

Greater Than a Tourist- San Juan Puerto Rico: 50 Travel Tips from a Local by Melissa Tait

Greater Than a Tourist – Lake George Area New York USA: 50 Travel Tips from a Local by Janine Hirschklau

Greater Than a Tourist – Monterey California United States: 50 Travel Tips from a Local by Katie Begley

Greater Than a Tourist – Chanai Crete Greece: 50 Travel Tips from a Local by Dimitra Papagrigoraki

Greater Than a Tourist – The Garden Route Western Cape Province South Africa: 50 Travel Tips from a Local by Li-Anne McGregor van Aardt

Greater Than a Tourist – Sevilla Andalusia Spain: 50 Travel Tips from a Local by Gabi Gazon

Children's Book: *Charlie the Cavalier Travels the World* by Lisa Rusczyk Ed. D.

91

> TOURIST

Follow us on Instagram for beautiful travel images:
http://Instagram.com/GreaterThanATourist

Follow *Greater Than a Tourist* on Amazon.

>Tourist Podcast
>T Website
>T Youtube
>T Facebook
>T Goodreads
>T Amazon
>T Mailing List
>T Pinterest
>T Instagram
>T Twitter
>T SoundCloud
>T LinkedIn
>T Map

> TOURIST

At *Greater Than a Tourist*, we love to share travel tips with you. How did we do? What guidance do you have for how we can give you better advice for your next trip? Please send your feedback to GreaterThanaTourist@gmail.com as we continue to improve the series. We appreciate your constructive feedback. Thank you.

METRIC CONVERSIONS

TEMPERATURE

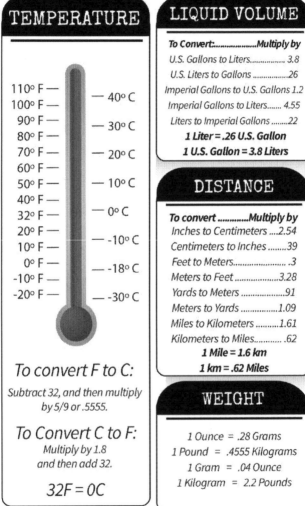

110° F	— 40° C
100° F	
90° F	— 30° C
80° F	
70° F	— 20° C
60° F	
50° F	— 10° C
40° F	
32° F	— 0° C
20° F	
10° F	— -10° C
0° F	
-10° F	— -18° C
-20° F	— -30° C

To convert F to C:

Subtract 32, and then multiply by 5/9 or .5555.

To Convert C to F:
Multiply by 1.8
and then add 32.

32F = 0C

LIQUID VOLUME

To Convert:..................Multiply by
U.S. Gallons to Liters................. 3.8
U.S. Liters to Gallons 26
Imperial Gallons to U.S. Gallons 1.2
Imperial Gallons to Liters....... 4.55
Liters to Imperial Gallons 22
1 Liter = .26 U.S. Gallon
1 U.S. Gallon = 3.8 Liters

DISTANCE

To convert ....Multiply by
Inches to Centimeters 2.54
Centimeters to Inches 39
Feet to Meters....................... .3
Meters to Feet 3.28
Yards to Meters 91
Meters to Yards 1.09
Miles to Kilometers 1.61
Kilometers to Miles............ .62
1 Mile = 1.6 km
1 km = .62 Miles

WEIGHT

1 Ounce = .28 Grams
1 Pound = .4555 Kilograms
1 Gram = .04 Ounce
1 Kilogram = 2.2 Pounds

TRAVEL QUESTIONS

- Do you bring presents home to family or friends after a vacation?

- Do you get motion sick?

- Do you have a favorite billboard?

- Do you know what to do if there is a flat tire?

- Do you like a sun roof open?

- Do you like to eat in the car?

- Do you like to wear sun glasses in the car?

- Do you like toppings on your ice cream?

- Do you use public bathrooms?

- Did you bring a cell phone and does it have power?

- Do you have a form of identification with you?

- Have you ever been pulled over by a cop?

- Have you ever given money to a stranger on a road trip?

- Have you ever taken a road trip with animals?

- Have you ever gone on a vacation alone?

- Have you ever run out of gas?

- If you could move to any place in the world, where would it be?

- If you could travel anywhere in the world, where would you travel?

- If you could travel in any vehicle, which one would it be?

- If you had three things to wish for from a magic genie, what would they be?

- If you have a driver's license, how many times did it take you to pass the test?

- What are you the most afraid of on vacation?

- What do you want to get away from the most when you are on vacation?

- What foods smell bad to you?

- What item do you bring on ever trip with you away from home?

- What makes you sleepy?

- What song would you love to hear on the radio when you're cruising on the highway?

- What travel job would you want the least?

- What will you miss most while you are away from home?

- What is something you always wanted to try?

- What is the best road side attraction that you ever saw?

- What is the farthest distance you ever biked?

- What is the farthest distance you ever walked?

- What is the weirdest thing you needed to buy while on vacation?

- What is your favorite candy?

- What is your favorite color car?

- What is your favorite family vacation?

- What is your favorite food?

- What is your favorite gas station drink or food?

- What is your favorite license plate design?

- What is your favorite restaurant?

- What is your favorite smell?

- What is your favorite song?

- What is your favorite sound that nature makes?

- What is your favorite thing to bring home from a vacation?

- What is your favorite vacation with friends?

- What is your favorite way to relax?

- Where is the farthest place you ever traveled in a car?

- Where is the farthest place you ever went North, South, East and West?

- Where is your favorite place in the world?

- Who is your favorite singer?

- Who taught you how to drive?

- Who will you miss the most while you are away?

- Who if the first person you will contact when you get to your destination?

- Who brought you on your first vacation?

- Who likes to travel the most in your life?

- Would you rather be hot or cold?

- Would you rather drive above, below, or at the speed limited?

- Would you rather drive on a highway or a back road?

- Would you rather go on a train or a boat?

- Would you rather go to the beach or the woods?

TRAVEL BUCKET LIST

1.

2.

3.

4.

5.

6.

7.

8.

9.

10.

NOTES

Printed in Great Britain
by Amazon